BIOMETRICS

Your Body and the Science of Security

Written by Maria Birmingham
Illustrated by Ian Turner

Owlkids Books

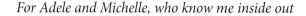

For Adele and Michelle, who know me inside out

Text © 2017 Maria Birmingham
Illustrations © 2017 Ian Turner

Owlkids Books acknowledges the financial support of the Canada Council for the Arts, the Ontario Arts Council, the Government of Canada through the Canada Book Fund (CBF) and the Government of Ontario through the Ontario Media Development Corporation's Book Initiative for our publishing activities.

Published in Canada by
Owlkids Books Inc.
10 Lower Spadina Avenue
Toronto, ON M5V 2Z2

Published in the United States by
Owlkids Books Inc.
1700 Fourth Street
Berkeley, CA 94710

Library and Archives Canada Cataloguing in Publication

Birmingham, Maria, author
      Biometrics : your body and the science of security / written by Maria Birmingham; illustrated by Ian Turner.

ISBN 978-1-77147-193-0 (hardcover)

      1. Biometry--Juvenile literature. 2. Biometric identification--Juvenile literature. I. Title.

QH323.5.B585 2017   j570.1'5195   C2017-900006-3

Library of Congress Control Number: 2016962529

Edited by: John Crossingham
Designed by: Danielle Arbour

Manufactured in Dongguan, China, in March 2017, by Toppan Leefung Packaging & Printing (Dongguan) Co., Ltd.
Job #BAYDC36

A   B   C   D   E   F

Publisher of Chirp, chickaDEE and OWL | Owlkids Books is a division of
www.owlkidsbooks.com

CONTENTS

IT'S A FACT:
THERE'S NO ONE LIKE YOU

You are one in a million.
Actually, if we include all the people roaming the planet, you're more like one in 7.4 *billion*. (But who's counting?) There are lots of things that make you stand out from the gigantic human crowd. Your ideas, values, and beliefs are an important part of what make you an individual.

Your physical features play a big role in your uniqueness, too. Each day, you're recognized as "you" because of the way you look. And you recognize those who are important in your life just the same way. For instance, when you spot a family member getting out of a car, you know that person immediately based on his or her appearance. And that person knows you just by glancing your way.

Now think about your fingerprints. No one else in the world has prints that match yours. The same goes for everyone else out there. Since the late 1800s, scientists have used fingerprints to accurately identify people.

It doesn't end with your physical appearance, though. You may recognize a friend from a distance based solely on the way he walks. You're familiar with the unique way he moves and know it almost instantly. A person's voice is also very distinctive. If your best friend calls you on the phone, chances are you'll know it's her as soon as you hear her voice.

We humans rely on our natural ability to recognize people by their many traits—both physical ones and aspects of behavior. Now we've entered a new era where computers are doing the same thing, analyzing our bodies and behaviors to identify us. This has turned the human body into a form of identification—an ID that we never forget to carry with us.

Biometrics is the name for the science of using the body to identify a person. The word "biometrics" comes from the Greek *bio* (meaning "life") and *metron* (meaning "measure"). This technology measures unique physical traits, such as our ear shape, scent, or vein patterns, to identify us. It can also ID us by analyzing how we perform a specific task, such as talking or typing.

As you read through these pages, you'll learn about topics like faceprints, voice recognition, and iris scanning. Yes, it sounds a lot like science fiction. But biometrics is really based on the age-old fact that there is no one else like you on Earth. And that makes your body the ultimate ID.

biometrics AT A GLANCE

Tablets like this throughout the book will give you a quick overview of each biometric.

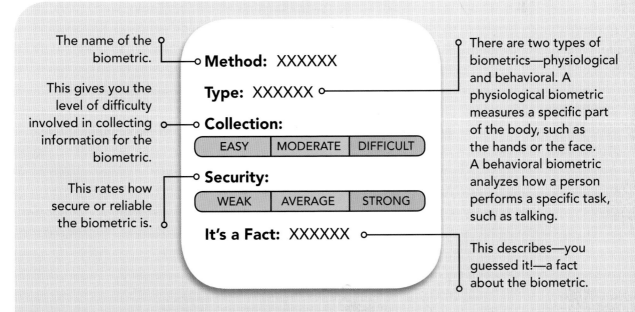

The name of the biometric.

This gives you the level of difficulty involved in collecting information for the biometric.

This rates how secure or reliable the biometric is.

Method: XXXXXX

Type: XXXXXX

Collection:

| EASY | MODERATE | DIFFICULT |

Security:

| WEAK | AVERAGE | STRONG |

It's a Fact: XXXXXX

There are two types of biometrics—physiological and behavioral. A physiological biometric measures a specific part of the body, such as the hands or the face. A behavioral biometric analyzes how a person performs a specific task, such as talking.

This describes—you guessed it!—a fact about the biometric.

WHY IDENTIFICATION?

So why is identification so important?

The bottom line is that it confirms we are who we say we are. It proves that we have the right to be in a certain place, do a certain thing, or receive a certain item or service. ID also protects our private information and belongings. In our daily lives, we need identification if we want to go to school, sign up for a sports team, visit the doctor, or travel outside the country. ID is sometimes necessary if we want to gain access to a building or to information on a computer.

WHO ARE YOU?

In ancient times, we identified a person by little more than his or her physical appearance. Over time, we've turned to stronger methods of ID, such as birth certificates and driver's licenses. These documents offer details like our birth date, a simple physical description, and even a photo. They're something you can hold in your possession and present to prove that you are you.

WHAT'S THE PASSWORD?

Passwords are another common form of ID. They're a word or a series of characters that are meant to be something only you know. Passwords allow us to access computers, devices, bank machines, social media accounts, and way more. But they have their own long history. Thousands of years ago, people relied on passwords to determine if someone was "one of them." For instance, a Roman soldier might have challenged a person to say the secret password—and prove he was an ally—before he could enter a particular region.

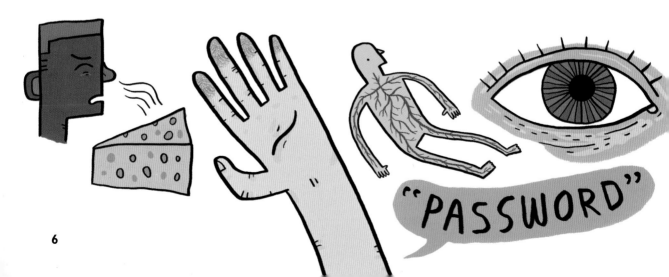

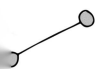

A HACKER ATTACK

While passwords and identification documents have been used successfully for years, they are far from perfect. Pieces of ID can be copied or faked. And there are more and more instances of passwords being cracked or stolen. In fact, in the past several years, tens of millions of passwords have been stolen by criminals hacking into the databases of major stores and banks. This has led to an increase in identity theft—when someone pretends to be somebody else. Identity theft allows thieves to get their hands on other people's private information, property, and money. It's a big problem. And this is where biometrics comes in.

WHO DO YOU THINK YOU ARE?

In the world of identification, biometrics is a game changer. Rather than depending on passwords or documents—things that you *know* or *own*, but that can be easily copied or stolen—biometrics focuses on who you *are*. Since your body and its specific traits are a part of you, they can't be misplaced or taken, and they're extremely difficult to duplicate. Biometrics takes advantage of the fact that no two people are exactly alike.

FOLLOW THESE STEPS

There are two stages involved in using biometrics to prove your identity. The first one is called *enrollment*. In this stage, a biometric system gets to know you for the first time by collecting a sample, such as a fingerprint or an iris pattern. During the second stage, called *verification*, identification is confirmed by comparing your original sample—known as the *template*—to another sample that you submit in the future.

THE MORE THE MERRIER

You may be wondering why there are so many different biometric methods. Isn't it enough to use, say, our fingerprints to prove our identity and call it a day? Why bother with our face, eyes, ears, hands, and so on? Well, for one thing, no biometric method is 100 percent foolproof. So experts continue to search for that one flawless method that'll leave all the others behind. But our curiosity may be the biggest reason for the growing interest in biometrics. Humans, especially scientists, are always on the lookout for an original idea. So when we come up with one, we just have to try it out to see how well it works!

Method: Fingerprint recognition

Type: Physiological

Collection:

EASY		

Security:

	AVERAGE	

It's a Fact: Used as identification for more than 100 years, making this the oldest biometric

WHEN YOUR FINGERS DO THE TALKING

While the concept of biometrics may be new to you, you're probably very familiar with the most common biometric method used to ID a person—fingerprinting. Those ridges found on the tips of your fingers form while you're growing inside your mom, and they remain the same throughout your lifetime. Every person has his or her own distinctive prints—even those of identical twins are different from one another. These fingerprint patterns are more than a series of fancy loops and whorls. In the world of biometrics, they are your own portable password, unlocking rooms, buildings, and devices.

HOW IT'S COLLECTED

Using ink pads and paper to collect fingerprints is so yesterday. High-tech scanners can now capture a digital fingerprint in the blink of an eye.

❶ A finger is placed on the scanner, allowing its print to be captured and analyzed.

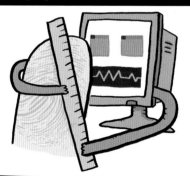

❷ A computer measures the distance and angles between the features in the fingerprint.

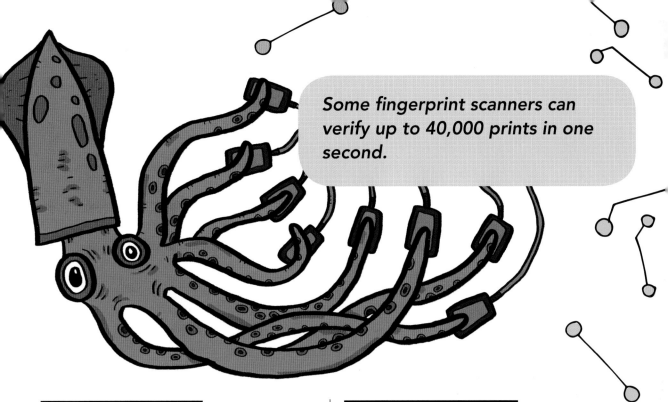

Some fingerprint scanners can verify up to 40,000 prints in one second.

CATCHING A BREAK

Tiny details within a fingerprint—called minutiae (say: ma-NU-she-ah)—are critical when it comes to identifying a person. These small breaks in the print's ridges are what make your fingerprints so unique. Computer software examines these minutiae to figure out whether one fingerprint matches another.

❸ In less than a second, this information is converted into a unique code that's stored in the machine.

WHERE IT ALL BEGAN

Throughout human history, fingerprints have been used as a type of signature. They were always considered a personal mark of an individual, but our ancient ancestors probably didn't realize that they could uniquely identify a person. The idea that no two fingerprints are exactly the same came about in the 1820s, when a Czech biologist named Jan Evangelista Purkinje made this observation. Even then, it took another sixty years before anyone suggested using fingerprints to ID an individual. That's when a Scottish doctor named Henry Faulds published an article about just that. Soon after, a system for classifying fingerprints was developed by the British scientist Francis Galton. His method of fingerprint identification is still used by experts to this day.

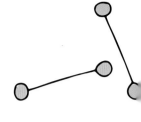

The Power of the Print

Having a form of ID right at your fingertips is certainly convenient. And it's fair to say that when they need to verify their identity, most people are more comfortable using their fingerprints than other body parts. That's probably because our prints are out in the open every day, and we're constantly using our hands. Scanning the tips of our fingers doesn't feel quite as unsettling as scanning, say, our eyeballs or our tongue. This is likely one of the reasons fingerprint recognition continues to be the most popular biometric in use today.

WHERE CAN YOU SEE IT?

Here are a few of the places where fingerprints have made their mark.

❶ A Canadian company designed a bike lock with a built-in fingerprint scanner. It will unlock only with the owner's print.

❷ Several smartphones and tablets use fingerprint verification to keep the devices secure.

❸ An American credit card has a built-in fingerprint scanner. The card can be used only after the cardholder swipes his finger across the sensor.

STILL TO COME?

• An American company is developing a scanner that will read fingerprints from a distance of 20 ft. (6 m) away. If successful, this could completely change the way that fingerprint scanning is done, allowing people to be identified without placing their fingers on a biometric sensor. While it sounds ultra-cool, this new technology does raise concerns about privacy. With this system, fingerprints could potentially be collected without a person even being aware that it's happening. And shouldn't we be able to choose when and if we want to share our ID with others?

• Scientists in South Korea have discovered a new way of analyzing fingerprints. It turns out we all have unique sweat pores on our fingertips. The experts hope to learn how to map the patterns of these pores so they may one day be used as identification.

PRINTS—YOU'RE COVERED IN 'EM

Fingerprints aren't the only identification marks on our skin. We also have distinctive patterns of ridges and grooves on our palms and the soles of our feet. It might surprise you to know that even the side of your hand has a unique print. Called the writer's palm (because it's the part that rests on paper as you write), this area is found along the outer side of your hand just below your baby finger. This print can also be used as a form of ID, though the tips of the fingers or thumbs are still the easiest prints to collect.

 **THE CONS**

▪ People who do a lot of physical work with their hands and anyone whose fingers are injured may have trouble matching their damaged prints to those on record.

▪ A fingerprint scanner may be fooled by fake prints. In December 2014, a German man took photos of a woman's hands from a distance. From there, he was able to make a replica of her thumbprint.

Method: Hand geometry recognition

Type: Physiological

Collection:

EASY		

Security:

	AVERAGE	

It's a Fact: Used to track attendance at schools and workplaces throughout the world

IT SURE COMES IN HANDY

It's not just your fingerprints and palm prints that make your hands unique. Every human hand has its own distinct characteristics. You can see this if you compare your hand to the hand of a friend. Sure, you both have four fingers and a thumb. But you'll notice slight differences in your hands' features, including width, finger length, and bone structure. These traits are enough to prove—hands down—that you are you.

HOW IT'S COLLECTED

Put 'er there! When it comes to ID, you just have to hand it to this biometric method.

❶ The hand is placed on a special plate, palm side down. The plate has five pegs that help to position the fingers properly.

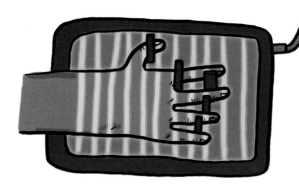

❷ A camera takes black-and-white pictures of the hand. It captures one image of the top of the hand and another from the side. Mirrors and reflectors help get all the necessary angles. Typically, three images of the hand are taken in sequence.

MAKING A MATCH

Even though our hand shape is unique, it's not quite as distinct as other physical traits, such as our fingerprints. For this reason, a hand geometry system is used not for identification but to verify that one hand sample matches another. That might make you think hand geometry is a weak biometric, but that's not the case. Hand geometry is accurate enough to verify whether someone has the right to enter a particular area, so it's a go-to choice in places such as airports and hospitals. And a big advantage this biometric has over others is that people are very accepting of it, since it's easy to use and most of us don't mind having our hands scanned.

READING BETWEEN THE LINES

Researchers at a university in Delhi, India, are studying another feature of our hands to see if it can be used as a form of ID: our knuckles. Just look at the skin patterns on yours. Lovely, aren't they? The knuckles feature plenty of lines, creases, wrinkles, and skin

Hand geometry biometrics first came along in the mid-1980s. That's when an American researcher named David Sidlauskas invented a scanning device that could measure the variations in hands and use this information as a form of ID.

folds. For the new biometric technique called *finger-knuckle-print* (or FKP, for short), researchers have designed a special system that scans the features of the knuckles. It takes digital images, which are then analyzed and stored in a computer system. The experts believe future knuckle "prints" could be compared to these original ones to accurately identify a person.

❸ Once an image is captured, as many as 31,000 points of the hand are analyzed by the scanner. Ninety different measurements are also taken, including the length of the fingers, the distance between the knuckles, and the width and thickness of the hand and fingers.

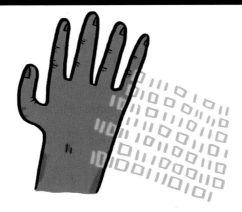

❹ This information is turned into a numerical code that's stored in the database of the scanner. It might *sound* like a lot of measuring, but the entire enrollment phase is done in about five seconds!

Put Your Hands Together for ID

Using hand geometry as a form of ID dates back some 31,000 years. Cave paintings from this time feature handprints. It's likely that these ancient prints were meant to be the artist's signature. Since handwriting didn't yet exist, the handprints provided proof of ID. Fast-forward to today, when using the human hand to verify identity has become a common biometric practice.

WHERE CAN YOU SEE IT?

Hand geometry systems are mainly used to provide access to secure areas in places such as banks. In some cases the entire hand is scanned, but in others only a finger is needed. With hand geometry systems, the scanner doesn't examine the fingerprint. Instead, it analyzes the unique features of the finger such as length and width. Here are a few examples of hand geometry systems in action.

❶ The so-called happiest place on Earth—aka Disney World—uses hand geometry scanners at the entrances to its parks.

❷ A high school in Philadelphia recently introduced a finger scanner that students must use before entering and exiting the school, to track who is in the building.

❸ Employees at a number of nuclear power plants in North America must use hand geometry readers to gain access to hazardous zones within the plants.

Even the thin skin found underneath your fingernails could one day be used to ID you. Your fingernail bed, which gives the nails its pink appearance, has unique ridges. Researchers are investigating the possibility of biometric authentication using the fingernail bed. This system would capture an image of these ridges and use their patterns as ID.

GET A GRIP

It turns out that the appearance of our hands may not be their only unique trait. Some experts are now looking at how a hand *functions* and trying to design a new technology called *hand-grip biometrics*. They believe that the way a person holds an object and the amount of pressure he uses to grip it is distinctive to each individual. In hand-grip biometrics, a special light analyzes the tissue and blood vessel patterns of a hand when it's gripping an object, such as a doorknob or a handheld device. These patterns are then used to create a record of an individual's distinctive grip to use for identification. In fact, researchers in the Netherlands are already working to develop objects that will ID their owners by their grip.

 # THE CONS

- Hand recognition systems have trouble identifying a person with wet hands or anyone wearing gloves.

- Rings can interfere with the accuracy of these systems.

- While adult hands don't generally change much over time, those of growing kids do. This makes the biometric less than perfect for identifying younger people.

- In cases of sickness or drastic weight change, the shape of the hand may alter, which affects the ability to ID a person.

FACIAL RECOGNITION

Method: Facial recognition

Type: Physiological

Collection:

| MODERATE |

Security:

| STRONG |

It's a Fact: Available on some gaming systems to log-in users

FACE
THE FACTS

Like most humans, you're an expert at recognizing a person simply by glancing at his or her face. Just think about all the faces you see in a day—parents, siblings, friends, teachers, your favorite celebrities, and the list goes on. Then consider how easily you can identify each one. You do it almost instantly. Experts figure the average person is able to recognize about 1,500 faces. And you've been able to distinguish between faces since long before you could talk. But facial recognition systems, which came on the scene in the 1960s, are catching up to your abilities. That said, you'd still reign victorious in a "face-off" with this biometric... for now.

HOW IT'S COLLECTED

Get face-to-face with a facial recognition system.

1 An image is taken using a camera. In some instances, an existing photo is scanned.

2 Computer software analyzes the image and measures the shape of specific features, or *nodal points*, on the face— these are things like the eyes, nose, cheekbones, and jawline. The software also tracks the distance between these points.

COMING SOON...IN 3D

There's room for improvement with any technology, including facial recognition. To make it more accurate, researchers are working on a system that will capture a 3D picture of a person using a set of three cameras. One points directly at an individual's face, another at the side of his or her face, and the third at an angle. With all three cameras working together, this system is able to spot subtle features, such as the curves of an eye socket or indentations in a chin, making it a more realistic ID.

FACES ON FILE

They say a picture is worth a thousand words. But a picture has the final word in facial biometrics. There are currently hundreds of millions of digital images filed away in facial recognition databases around the world. And they can all be used to ID a person—whether it's for something as simple as tagging someone in a photo or for the more serious business of catching a criminal. The

IT'S IN THE SKIN

In some instances, such as poor lighting conditions, facial recognition technology can't capture a faceprint that's precise enough for ID. But that problem might be solved by a new biometric method called skin texture analysis. With this technique, a photo is taken of a patch of skin. This *skinprint* captures the lines, patterns, pores, and spots on the skin—similar to a fingerprint. A computer then analyzes these features and uses the skinprint as a form of ID. Combining skin texture analysis with facial recognition software could create a stronger and more reliable biometric.

images in these archives come from just about anywhere, including passports and driver's licenses. Social media is also an important source for these databases. Since many people regularly post photos of themselves and their friends and family on sites like Facebook, Instagram, and Twitter, there are countless images available for facial recognition archives. For some people, the existence of all these images is concerning. After all, many of us don't even realize that our faceprints are out in the world, or that they may be used one day to identify us without our permission.

❸ This information is turned into a unique mathematical code, which is known as a *faceprint*. It's essentially a map of the face.

A Face in the Crowd

With most biometric methods, you enroll, or register, with a recognition system. But that's not necessarily the case with facial recognition. Enrollment can take place without your knowledge. Sometimes your faceprint is captured while you're out in the world simply enjoying your day. Special video cameras have been set up in certain public places to monitor people. Using facial recognition software, these cameras pick out your face from a crowd, run your faceprint through a database, and try to determine your identity—whether you like it or not.

WHERE
CAN YOU SEE IT?

Facial recognition systems are already in use in airports around the world. Security services use these methods to identify passengers who are traveling with fake passports. And facial biometrics has long been used by police departments to match faceprints to images already in their databases. Here are some other places you might spot the biometric.

❶ Some televisions include facial recognition software. You enroll each family member's face into the system. When the TV is turned on, it recognizes the person watching and chooses a show based on his or her preferences. In a way, the TV watches you!

❷ Chinese engineers have invented a bank machine that scans faces to identify customers rather than asking for a password.

❸ At one Canadian department store, facial recognition cameras are in place throughout the building. Faceprints captured by the cameras are compared to images in the store's database to help ID past shoplifters.

An American company is working on technology that will turn simple facial expressions—like a wink or a scrunched nose—into a code that'll unlock devices.

HOW WILL YOU BE PAYING— CASH, CREDIT, OR FACE?

Leave the wallet behind. A Finnish company recently began working on a scanner that will let you pay with your face. Instead of using cash or credit cards, you simply position your face in front of a scanner. (Smile!) Once ID is confirmed through facial recognition, you can go ahead and make a purchase. The system links up to your file in its database to charge you for your items.

MONKEYING AROUND

Facial recognition is useful even in the animal kingdom. To help with their research into primate behavior, German scientists used the biometric in a local zoo to monitor twenty-four chimpanzees. They found that the recognition system was excellent at identifying each animal. This saved the researchers time, since they didn't have to spend hours analyzing photos or videos to observe each chimp. Word is that this technology could eventually be used in the wild to track chimps. And it might be helpful for identifying other species, like zebras or cheetahs, through their unique body markings.

 **THE CONS**

- Systems have a hard time interpreting facial expressions. When someone smiles, for instance, it changes the shape of the face. Since the smiling face isn't an exact match to the one in the database, the system may not be able to verify ID.

- Slight changes in a person's appearance—such as facial hair, makeup, glasses, a hat, or a different hairstyle—can throw off a facial biometric system.

- Poor lighting can affect a system's ability to distinguish a face.

- Most systems struggle to identify someone from her profile; they prefer an image of somebody who's facing forward.

- It's challenging for systems to distinguish between identical twins.

RICS BIOMETRICS BIOMETRICS BIOMETRICS BIOMETRICS BIOMETRICS BIOMETRICS BIOMETRICS BIOMETRICS BIO

THE DOWNSIDE OF
BIOMETRICS

Interest in biometrics really got going about forty years ago. Today, it's hard to keep up with the technology, especially since researchers are continually working to find the next best thing in ID. While experts are focused on the possibilities for and future of biometrics, many people have concerns about the technology itself.

PRIVACY PLEASE

The biggest concern about biometrics is its effect on privacy. Opponents of biometrics worry about the fact that ID can be collected without a person's knowledge. Few people like to feel as if they're being watched or tracked as they live their lives. Privacy is a right we all deserve. It should be up to us to decide when or even if we share with others information about our lives and our habits. Some biometrics take away this right to privacy.

For instance, some facial recognition cameras have been set up in public areas. Once these cameras capture a faceprint, this data can be used to identify you. It allows somebody to track your whereabouts. It's also possible that your ID would be shared with others without your permission. And you have absolutely no say in any of this. For many people, this situation is simply unacceptable.

NOW YOU SEE IT...

Aside from the privacy issues, some people are uncomfortable with the idea of having so much personal biometric data out in the world. They fear that as our ID sits filed away in various databases, individuals could hack into these systems and gain access to our information. If they're successful, then what? After all, we can change a stolen password or replace a driver's license, but we can't exactly rustle up new fingerprints or retinas! What would happen if someone got his hands on our unique biometric ID?

ACCESS DENIED

Another drawback is that no biometric method is completely foolproof. While errors are uncommon, there is always a chance that a biometric device will fail to recognize an individual. This technical malfunction would make the person's biometric ID useless. In these cases, the person would likely have to prove his identity in another way—by using a document like a driver's license, for instance. But isn't biometrics supposed to replace these types of ID? And if they don't, then what's the point?

TIME WILL TELL

In spite of these issues, many companies and governments believe in biometrics. They consider it to be a reliable way to protect secure areas, computer networks and files, and personal devices like smartphones. And they argue that biometric methods will only get more dependable as the technology advances. This will help reduce the number of errors and the possibility of somebody hacking into the system. And to be fair, even our current methods of ID, like passwords, aren't without problems. They regularly face threats from hackers. In the end, it's ultimately up to us— society itself—to decide where and how biometrics should be used.

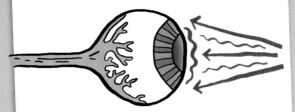

Method: Iris recognition

Type: Physiological

Collection:

> EASY

Security:

> STRONG

It's a Fact: Said to be the most accurate biometric method available to date

While fingerprints have about seventy unique features that help with identification, the iris has more than triple this amount.

THE EYES
HAVE IT

There's a saying that the eyes are the window to the soul—they show you who a person really is, deep down inside. But in the world of biometrics, the eyes are a window to your identity. So much so that there are two biometric methods that use the eye as a form of ID—iris recognition and retinal scanning.

MY, WHAT UNIQUE EYES YOU HAVE

When you talk about the color of your eyes, you're referring to your iris. This ring of colored tissue that surrounds your pupil controls the amount of light that's allowed into the eye. But your iris also sets you apart from those around you. Take a close look and you'll see that there's much more to your iris than its color. Each of your irises has its own pattern, including rings, spots, and speckles that make it unique. It's these complex patterns that help put the "eye" in ID.

HOW IT'S COLLECTED

Come in close and get an eyeful of an iris scanner.

❶ Sunglasses must be removed before a scan. But eyeglasses and contact lenses aren't a problem.

❷ A user stands 3 to 10 in. (7.6 to 25.4 cm) from a specially designed camera.

❸ The camera takes a picture of the iris. Then a computer examines the pattern, mapping out nearly 250 unique features.

❹ The computer uses mathematical calculations to create a code for the iris. This code is stored within a database.

OUT OF SIGHT ID

You'll have to venture all the way to the very back of your eyeball to find your retina. The retina is the thin tissue that lines the back of the eye and processes light, allowing you to see. Despite it being hidden away inside your head, it's just as helpful as your iris in identifying you. A network of blood vessels runs through the retina, creating a branch-like pattern. By mapping the arrangement of these vessels, experts can quickly nail down your ID.

Method: Retinal scanning

Type: Physiological

Collection:

		DIFFICULT

Security:

		STRONG

It's a Fact: Chance of a retinal scan making an ID error is only one in 10 million

HOW IT'S COLLECTED

Look into the light to see a retinal scanner in action.

❶ A retinal scanner is typically found outside a door leading to a secure area. Before a scan, a user must remove her glasses or contact lenses.

❷ She places her eye very close to the scanning device—about 0.5 in. (1.3 cm) away—and aligns it with the lens.

❸ Staring at a specific point of light within the lens, she must keep her head motionless for about ten to fifteen seconds and avoid blinking.

❹ A low-energy beam of light shines deep into the eye, capturing a digital image of the pattern of blood vessels. The scanner measures over 400 points to get an accurate image. It takes three to five scans to ensure an image is usable.

❺ The results are converted into a computer code and stored in a database to be used in the future to verify ID.

One of the benefits of using the retina for ID is that it's found inside the body, where it's protected. Unless it's afflicted by disease, the retina is thought to remain unchanged for our entire lives.

IRIS RECOGNITION

IT'S ALL ABOUT
EYE-DENTITY

How do they stack up against each other? Let's look a little more closely at iris recognition and retinal scanning.

WHERE CAN YOU SEE IT?

Iris scanning is used by companies around the world to grant access to rooms and computerized information. And hundreds of airports also use iris scanners. Here are some other examples.

❶ Iris scanners are sometimes used to identify horses. This allows for much more humane treatment, since it replaces the need to brand or mark the horses for identification.

❷ Some cars use iris recognition for ID. When a driver gets into the car, she looks in the rearview mirror and scans her iris. The iris must match an image stored in the database for her to be able to start the car.

❸ An American company has designed a smartwatch with a built-in iris scanner. The watch can be linked to everything from computers to door locks. An iris pattern becomes the password to unlock these items.

Researchers at Carnegie Mellon University in Pennsylvania are developing a camera that can rapidly take iris scans of every person in a room from about 40 ft. (12 m) away.

👎 THE CONS

- Accidents or diseases involving the eye can make it challenging to ID an individual using the iris.

- Experts have long believed that the pattern of the iris remains the same throughout a person's lifetime. But researchers at a university in Indiana have recently found that the iris may change as we age.

- A German researcher proved that an iris scanner isn't foolproof. He used life-size photographs of several people's eyes to fool, or spoof, a scanner.

24

Researchers in Dresden, Germany, are working on a portable retinal scanner that will be small enough to fit inside a pocket, for on-the-go ID.

WHERE CAN YOU SEE IT?

Retinal scanning is used for security by many government agencies, including the FBI. Here are some of the other ways it's a real eye-opener.

1 A hotel in Boston has retinal scanning devices mounted on the walls outside each room. A guest can open the door with his or her eye. No key required!

2 A Chinese manufacturer launched a smartphone with a built-in retinal scanner that's used to unlock the device.

3 The government of the United Arab Emirates has created a drone to deliver packages across the country. A retinal recognition system on the drone ensures that each package ends up with its rightful owner.

RETINAL SCANNING

 THE CONS

■ Retinal scans require a person to concentrate for a prolonged period of time. Enrolling with the system can take over a minute.

■ Some consider retinal scans an unpleasant experience, since the eye has to be positioned so close to the scanner.

■ Many believe that the light from the scanner can harm the eye. Although this isn't true, it makes some people hesitant to use the technology.

IRIS RECOGNITION VS. RETINAL SCANNING

- Both methods are fast and accurate.
- Both have a high security level, since iris and retina patterns are unique to each individual.
- Retinal scanning is considered invasive because users have to place their eyes so close to the device.

VERDICT: While both are strong biometrics, iris scanning has an easier method of collection, making it a more widely accepted choice for identification.

VOICE RECOGNITION

Method: Voice recognition

Type: Physiological & Behavioral

Collection:

EASY		

Security:

		STRONG

It's a Fact: More than 65 million voiceprints are said to be stored in databases worldwide

TALK THE TALK

Read this sentence aloud. Hear that? Your voice has a lot to say. Not only does it help you communicate, but it's also distinctive enough to be used to ID you. Think about how easily you're able to identify your friends, family members, and even your favorite singers by nothing but the sound of their voice. And others recognize the sweet sound of you as well. Of course, when it comes to the voice, there's one big benefit in using it for identification: it's easy. Just open your mouth and speak up!

HOW IT'S COLLECTED

No need to talk it over. Read on to learn about the technology behind voice recognition.

❶ A person's voice is recorded as she says certain words or phrases. About eight seconds of speech is all that's needed. This recording can be done over a telephone.

❷ A computer turns the recording into a unique coded form known as a *voiceprint*. This voiceprint is a record of the speaker's unique sound and rhythm.

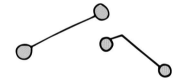

Voice recognition should not be confused with speech recognition. Speech recognition is all about recognizing words as they are spoken. For example, a digital assistant found on certain phones and tablets uses speech recognition to recognize what is being said. But only a voice recognition system can identify who is speaking.

THAT'S YOUR BODY TALKING

So why is your voice so unique, and what makes it sound different from the voice of, say, your parents or siblings? To begin with, your voice has its own tone and volume. And then there's the size and shape of your mouth, throat, teeth, tongue, lips, and jaw—all these determine the sound of your voice. In addition, the shape of your vocal cords and voice box, as well as the way your mouth moves, helps to create that distinct sound of yours. Finally, you can't help learning a certain style of speaking from those around you as you grow up.

A WINNING COMBINATION

With so many factors involved in creating your voice, it makes for an unusual biometric. Unlike most other systems, voice recognition is both a physiological *and* a behavioral biometric. As a physiological biometric, it identifies a person by relying on certain physical characteristics that help produce speech, including the voice box and throat. But it's also a behavioral biometric because it analyzes the way a person speaks, taking note of details such as how he pronounces words and the motion of his mouth.

Let That Voice Be Heard

The roots of voice recognition go back to the 1960s, when scientists first analyzed how people made particular sounds of speech. By the 1970s, the first voice recognition systems were developed. Today, there are millions of voiceprints stored in databases around the globe. And researchers say this number is on its way up … *way up*. They predict that in several years, 5 billion people will have created a voiceprint that'll be filed away in a database somewhere.

WHERE
CAN YOU SEE IT?

Voice recognition systems are used by governments and companies, including banks, around the globe to help people gain access to secure information over the telephone. One of the big benefits to this is that individuals don't need to be physically present to retrieve their data. Take a listen to some of the other uses for voice biometrics.

❶ One company has designed a journal that opens using voice recognition. It lets out an alarm if someone other than the owner tries to access it.

❷ A high-tech community in Pennsylvania uses voice recognition to grant people access to buildings within the area.

❸ A German company has created a voice biometric system that can be used by doctors to access patients' medical files over the phone.

SNIFFLES AND SECURITY

Here's something to think about: Could the common cold fool a voice recognition system? After all, when your nose is stuffed and your throat is scratchy, you don't sound much like yourself. It turns out the answer is no. When a voiceprint is created, up to fifty different characteristics are measured. These include qualities such as the amount of vibration in your voice, its tone, and the length of sounds in your speech. A recognition system analyzes all these specific traits, not just the sound of your voice. So it can recognize you even if you're a sniffling, coughing mess. In fact, the biometric is able to recognize you even if you suddenly start speaking another language!

IS THAT REALLY YOU?

Okay, so a cold doesn't trick a voice recognition system, but what about a person who imitates voices perfectly? Could he pull a fast one on the biometric? Amazingly, that's a no again! An impersonator may sound like an exact match to your ears, but he can't capture all the characteristics that make up a voiceprint. The sounds and speech patterns we produce depend on the unique shape of our vocal tract—that is, the mouth, throat, tongue, and lips. So while a person may be able to create a perfect imitation of a voice, a recognition system can decipher the tiniest differences to determine that it's not the real deal.

FOR THE RECORD

So … let's review. A cold? Can't dupe a voice recognition system. An impersonator? Not a chance. What about a voice recording? That'll be strike three. Whenever a voice is recorded, its sound is changed ever so slightly in the process. A voice recognition system can detect this minor change. And this ultimately prevents people from being able to fool, or spoof, the biometric and get access to private information.

THE CONS

• Our voices can change as we age, so a voiceprint created by a younger person may not be a match as she grows older.

• The type of phone used may affect accuracy. For instance, if someone enrolled with a home telephone and then used a cell phone to verify his ID, the system may not be able to match the voices.

• Background noise or a bad connection may affect some systems.

Method: Vein recognition

Type: Physiological

Collection:

EASY		

Security:

		STRONG

It's a Fact: Vein patterns are virtually impossible to forge

GETTING UNDER YOUR SKIN

It's hard to believe that something hidden inside your body could be of any help in identifying you. But your veins have a story to tell. They create patterns below the skin's surface—sort of like your body's own road map. These vein patterns are unique to you, just as your fingerprints are different from everyone else's. When it comes time to reveal your identity using your veins, it's as simple as analyzing these branch-like patterns in your fingers, on your palm, or on the back of your hand.

HOW IT'S COLLECTED

It's time to shine a light on the secrets behind vein recognition.

❶ A finger or hand is placed on the vein scanner.

❷ The scanner shines a special light onto the finger or hand. (This light is the same as that used in a TV's remote control.) Red blood cells in the veins absorb the light, but the rest of the hand does not.

❸ A camera records a digital image. In this image, the veins appear like black lines, since they have absorbed the light. The rest of the hand appears white. This vein pattern map is then stored in a database.

WHERE

CAN YOU SEE IT?

Here are a few of the ways that vein patterns are being used as identifiers.

❶ A North American biometric company uses vein scanners on school buses. They capture the vein patterns in kids' palms when they board or exit a bus, keeping track of the students.

❷ Several companies have created a computer mouse that has a built-in palm vein scanner. A user places her hand above the device to unlock it.

❸ Vein-scanning terminals have been introduced at a university in Sweden. At stores and restaurants on campus, students can pay for purchases by scanning their hands.

HE SAW THE LIGHT

Using vein patterns as a biometric was the brainchild of a British engineer named Joseph Rice. He came up with the idea in 1984, while he was driving home from work. As sunlight shone on his hands, he noticed the pattern made by the veins below his skin. This got Rice wondering if vein patterns might be used as a form of ID. So he built a vein scanner and tested his prototype on his coworkers. Rice discovered that everyone's vein patterns are different, and they don't change from week to week. He even scanned the veins of identical twins and found they also had unique patterns. Today's vein recognition systems are based on Rice's early prototype.

 **THE CONS**

▪ The quality of a scan can be affected by factors like an individual's body temperature, the temperature in the room itself, or how close the veins are to the skin's surface.

Even the vein patterns in your eyes are unique. A biometric called eye-vein recognition captures an eyeprint of the sclera—the white outer layer of the eye. These eyeball selfies allow the sclera's veins to be used as ID.

BIOMETRICS OF THE FUTURE?

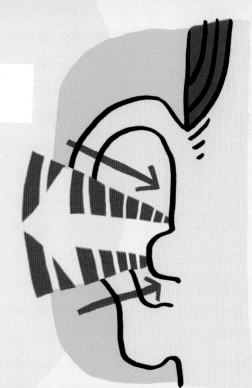

You can be certain that researchers are working away on new biometric methods even as you're reading this. Here are a few of the most interesting technologies in development. Some are in their earliest stages. Others may never see the light of day. But it's still fun to imagine what might be!

NOW EAR THIS

During the 1880s, a French police officer named Alphonse Bertillon suggested that a person's ear shape could be used for identification. All these years later, ear recognition is finally in the works. This biometric relies on scanning and measuring ear features, especially the outer rim, known as the helix. This area is believed to have distinct curves and ridges that set each person apart from the rest of the population. For now, experts say the technology behind ear recognition is too slow to be used on its own. But it might be used alongside another biometric as a method of ID.

LISTEN UP

In other ear news, researchers at a university in England are looking inside the ear for a possible new biometric. When sound enters your ear, tiny nerve cells deep inside react to the noise. These cells generate a faint sound, like an echo, that can be picked up only by a supersensitive microphone. The researchers believe every person's ear creates its own unique sound, meaning an individual could be identified by her "ear noise." For this to work, a series of sounds would be sent through a phone line and the sound pattern produced by the ear would be analyzed.

THE BOTTOM LINE

Japanese engineers are working on a car seat that identifies you by your bum. Yup, bum recognition! The seat comes equipped with nearly 400 sensors that detect the shape of an individual's bottom once he sits down. A 3D image of the bum is then sent to a computer and stored in its database. The next time that person sits in the car, the biometric system analyzes his behind to see if it matches the one on record. If it does, the car will start, eliminating the need for a key. A perfect anti-theft device!

JUST BREATHE

A team of researchers in Switzerland recently started sniffing around the possibility of breath biometrics. Using a special device, the scientists analyzed the breath of eleven volunteers several times a day. After repeating this over the course of nine days, the experts found that every individual has a unique breathprint. This natural odor can be used to distinguish one person from another, which suggests that our breath could be used as a password to unlock our devices.

WALK THIS WAY

Experts have found that your walk, or gait, is distinct enough to be used as an identifier. Gait recognition analyzes and IDs a person's walking style, paying particular attention to how the shoulders, arms, knees, and feet move. In some cases, a camera is used to examine the motion of the body. Researchers also use invisible radio waves to track a person. As he walks, the radio waves are directed at him. Since everyone has a distinct walking style, these waves bounce back differently for each person. This data can then be used for identification.

33

Method: Signature recognition

Type: Behavioral

Collection:
| EASY | | |

Security:
| | MODERATE | |

It's a Fact: Mostly used at banks and other financial institutions

THE WRITE
STUFF

A signature is one of the fastest ways to say: I was here. And that personalized scribble is also a telltale sign of your identity. Written signatures have been used as identifiers since the late 1800s, when trained experts analyzed handwriting and tried to match one signature to another by noting their similarities. Today, computers have taken over this role. But to confirm ID, these systems examine signatures in real time, that is, at the very moment they are being made.

HANDWRITING THROUGH HISTORY

The signature itself has been an identifying mark for humans for thousands of years. Take a look at its evolution:

• Cave paintings from 31,000 years ago were "signed" with handprints, since early humans didn't write.

• In Babylon around 500 BCE, fingerprints were pressed onto clay tablets to "sign" business contracts.

• Around 300 BCE, thumbprints were used in China as signatures on documents.

• Until the Middle Ages, wax seals were sometimes used to sign documents.

IT'S NOT WHAT IT LOOKS LIKE

When it comes to identifying a signature, you might think that all those loops and swirls hold the key. But in signature recognition, the actual appearance of the signature is only *part* of the story. What's more important is how the signature is made. As someone is signing her name, a recognition system analyzes several specific factors, such as changes in speed and rhythm of the writing, the spacing of the letters, the direction of the writing, the number of times the pen is lifted, and the pressure applied to the tablet by the pen. If those details match what's already in the system, the computer makes a positive ID. It's more about how she writes her signature than what she writes that reveals identity.

SIGN HERE

You've probably seen someone signing an electronic signature pad, but that doesn't necessarily mean that you've

HOW IT'S COLLECTED

Forget about putting pen to paper. In *signature recognition*, things have gone digital.

❶ An individual uses a pen called a stylus to sign her name on a special writing tablet.

❷ This signature is converted into digital form so it can be recorded and analyzed by a computer.

witnessed signature biometrics in action. For instance, your mom might sign an electronic pad at a store when she's making a purchase. In this case, the system is only capturing an image of her signature to authorize the transaction. It's not identifying your mom. In signature biometrics, on the other hand, the system analyzes the pattern of motion as a person signs her name and uses this information to confirm ID.

• Before the eighteenth century, the majority of people could not write. Legal documents were often signed with an *X* instead of a signature.

• In the 1800s, more people learned to read and write, so handwritten signatures became more common.

• In the late 1970s, signature recognition systems were developed.

• Today in China, Japan, Taiwan, and Korea, people sometimes use a stamp-like object called a name seal instead of writing their signature. Each person has his or her own personal seal. In fact, these signature seals were first used in East Asia starting around 220 BCE.

SIGNATURE RECOGNITION

Where Do I Sign?

One of the biggest advantages of signature biometrics is that people tend to be very accepting of it and are quite comfortable having their signature collected for identification. That's probably because we're used to scribbling it down on a regular basis at stores, banks, and so on. And it also helps that signing our name is something we do rather than something that is part of us— like, say, our eyes or hands. Our signature is easy to share.

WRITE THIS WAY

You may be wondering if it's possible for someone to forge, or imitate, a signature to fool a recognition system. After all, you've probably heard stories about people copying someone else's signature for their own selfish reasons—maybe on a test or permission form, for instance. But it turns out that it's very difficult for an imposter to fool a signature recognition system. While he or she may forge the look of a signature perfectly, it's nearly impossible to copy the *way* a person signs his or her name.

GETTING IT WRONG

While we may be comfortable *using* signature recognition, it isn't always as reliable as other biometric systems. Signature recognition is a behavioral biometric (meaning it's all about how we do something), and behaviors can often change. If we're extremely tired, for instance, or if a writing tablet is awkwardly placed, our handwriting may take on a different look. For this reason, a recognition system may not always be able to verify a signature. To get around this issue, signature recognition is often combined with a password to give the biometric added security.

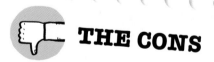 THE CONS

- Signature recognition is not useful for injured or aging people who can't write their signature well enough to be read by the system.

- The method is not appropriate for people who are unable to write.

KEY IT IN

Some of us spend more time typing on a computer than writing on paper. But as luck would have it, there's a biometric for that, too! Researchers discovered that the way a person types is as individual as his or her handwriting. Enter keystroke dynamics. This biometric examines factors such as the speed of typing and how a person uses specific keys. In particular, keystroke dynamics focuses on two things:

Dwell time: length of time a key is pressed

Flight time: time between releasing one key and pressing the next one

In keystroke biometrics, software analyzes an individual's typing pattern. And this pattern is then evaluated in the future to ID the person. One of the big problems with this technology is that, much like writing, a person's typing can vary from moment to moment. If he is tired, frustrated, or speaking to someone as he types, the rhythm of his typing may be affected. Even so, several European companies rely on this biometric for computer access.

Keyboard dynamics dates back to the Second World War. At that time, the military communicated using Morse code—a system of sending messages that uses sounds or dots and dashes to represent letters and numbers. Experts learned to ID a person based on her unique rhythm of typing Morse code. In some cases, they could even determine if the sender was an ally or an enemy.

ODOR RECOGNITION

Method: Odor recognition

Type: Physiological

Collection:

		DIFFICULT

Security:

UNKNOWN

It's a Fact: Relies on scent sensors that imitate the human nose

FOLLOW
THAT NOSE

We all have an odor. We can't help it. Of course, there's that stink that comes after playing an intense game of basketball or hockey. But there's also a smell we emit all day long. This subtle, natural scent comes from about thirty chemicals produced by the body. No matter how much you scrub your body clean, that scent pattern is there to stay. And it's uniquely yours. No one else has your *smellprint*. Although it's still in the research stages, odor recognition aims to detect an individual's scent and use it to ID him with a device called an electronic nose, or e-nose.

HOW IT'S COLLECTED

When it comes to ID, odor recognition is the ultimate sniff test.

❶ Special sensors in the e-nose detect odor molecules.

❷ A signal is sent to a computer program, which then works to ID the smell by analyzing scent patterns, or the arrangement of the chemicals that make up the odor.

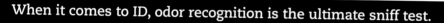

Sniff
sniff

PUP POWER

If this sounds far out, let's remember that identifying people by their scent is nothing new. For centuries, bloodhounds have been used by humans to track down lost people and criminals. These dogs have a remarkable sense of smell. They can trail a person for miles in all types of weather after simply getting a whiff of his or her odor on an item, like an article of clothing.

THIS NOSE KNOWS

Researchers at Spain's Technical University of Madrid were inspired by the bloodhound and its keen sense of smell in their work. They designed an e-nose prototype that can accurately ID a person's odor. An individual places her hand inside a small glass jar. The e-nose then sniffs the hand to determine its unique smellprint. This print is stored in a database to be used in the future for identification. While the e-nose device is not as skilled as a bloodhound yet, it can identify a person accurately about 85 percent of the time. And it's had some success filtering out other scents, like perfumes or hand creams, which may interfere with a person's natural odor. For now, the researchers say the e-nose is most useful alongside another biometric, like iris recognition or fingerprint scanning. But they believe it may one day work perfectly well on its own.

You leave your scent behind on everything you touch. That's the reason a bloodhound is able to pick up your trail.

THE SHAPE OF THINGS TO COME

Your natural scent is not your only nasal identifier—even your nose itself can help to ID you. Researchers at the University of Bath in England have found that your nose shape is distinct and can be picked out from a crowd. They've created a system that scans a nose and analyzes its shape. According to the researchers, this scanning system looks at three specific characteristics: the nose's length, its width at the tip, and its width between the eyes. It then uses these details to match the nose with information already in a database to identify an individual. The researchers suggest that this biometric method would be useful to ID people in crowded areas, like airports or shopping malls, because the nose can be easily analyzed from a distance. Of course, one of the issues is that a person can change the shape of his or her nose through surgery. In these cases, this ID technique would be useless. Or you could say it'd suffer a complete nosedive!

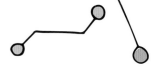

May I Smell You?

Since most of us would rather not share our scent with others, it may seem as if odor recognition is doomed to fail. But it's likely that this method of ID will become more acceptable as time goes on. That's because as the technology advances, it will become possible to identify people as they walk past an e-nose. This would mean that an individual wouldn't need to stop and be sniffed. And with that extra step out of the way, people will probably be more willing to use odor recognition as a form of identification.

WHERE
CAN YOU SEE IT?

Odor recognition biometrics is still a work in progress. But there are some interesting ideas for how the technology might use your personal scent down the road.

❶ One credit card company is considering placing a person's smellprint on a card. A sensor would have to match the odor of the person with the scent on the card before a purchase was approved.

❷ A British company is developing a scent-detecting system for computers that will sniff the back of a person's hand to verify identity.

❸ Some experts think a person's smellprint could be included on a passport. A passenger would walk past a sensor at the airport to match his body odor to the scent on the passport.

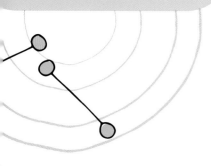

SMELL YA LATER!

Even as researchers try to fine-tune the technology behind odor recognition, they're already thinking about the future of the biometric. There's talk that odor recognition might become advanced enough to identify a person from a distance. This would be helpful in specific cases. For instance, police could detect and arrest a dangerous criminal by capturing his scent from afar.

Just as interesting is the idea that odor biometrics might be used to ID a person's smellprint days after she has left a location. This "scent signature" could help law enforcement officers sniff out a missing person or even identify someone who has fled the scene of a crime.

BEYOND ID

E-noses can be used for tasks other than identification. For one thing, they have the ability to uncover medical issues like infections and diseases. Certain illnesses can be noticed in changes to a person's breath—for example, a fruity odor could be a sign of diabetes. And certain e-noses can detect these scents and diagnose the problems causing them.

An e-nose has even made its way to outer space! NASA installed an e-nose aboard the International Space Station. But this nose wasn't sniffing astronauts—instead, it used its thirty-two sensors to detect dangerous odors and chemicals in the air.

 THE CONS

- Using body odor as ID makes some people uncomfortable. (We don't usually go around smelling other people or allowing them to smell us!)
- There are concerns that perfumes, deodorants, and other human-made smells may mask your natural odor and affect the biometric's accuracy.
- Body odor may be altered by factors like mood, illness, and the foods you eat, possibly interfering with the biometric's ability to do its job.

THERE'S MORE
IN STORE

You never know what new and unusual biometric methods are around the corner. Here are a few more innovative technologies to keep on your radar.

SAY "AHHHH..."

No two tongues are exactly alike—each one has distinctive bumps and ridges. With this in mind, researchers in Hong Kong have designed a tongue scanner that records a 3D image of a person's tongue and analyzes qualities such as texture, color, length, and thickness. The person can then be identified using this *tongueprint*. The researchers suggest this biometric could be a useful form of ID at airports and banks. Simply stick out your tongue in front of a camera and... ID verified!

DNA ID

Perhaps nothing about us is as unique as our DNA (that's a molecule found in each cell that tells the body how to develop). For decades, researchers have used DNA biometrics to identify individuals by analyzing samples of hair, fingernails, skin, saliva, or blood. But DNA identification typically must be done in a laboratory, and it takes days to get results. This makes it a poor choice in situations where you need to identify someone quickly. That's about to change, though. A California professor recently developed a handheld device that can be used anywhere to ID a person's DNA in less than ninety minutes.

LEAVE IT TO THE LIPS

Scientists in Poland and Taiwan are zeroing in on the lips as a possible way of identifying individuals. They've designed a recognition system that scans lips, focusing on their size, shape, and distinctive features to confirm ID. In similar studies, researchers in Sweden are considering the possibility of lip-movement recognition. This biometric involves watching how lips move as a person says certain words or letters, and then using this movement to identify him or her.

THAT SIGNATURE SMILE

A smile may say it all, according to a team of researchers at a university in New York. They're studying smile recognition, which examines the facial changes that happen when we grin. The team snaps a series of photos of a person as she's smiling. Then a computer analyzes the changing muscles and lines in the skin around the mouth. This allows the experts to create "smile maps" that are said to distinguish one person from another.

PUT YOUR FOOT DOWN

Scientists at a university in Japan are putting one foot in front of the other as they develop a new technology called *foot pressure biometrics*. The experts studied 104 barefoot volunteers and analyzed the movement of their heels, soles, and toes as they walked on a pressure-sensitive mat. They found it was possible to correctly ID a person using footstep patterns over 99 percent of the time. And they say this technology could one day help identify people at airports, banks, and other secure buildings.

BIOMETRICS: WHAT CAN WE EXPECT?

If you think about it, biometrics got its start thousands of years ago. Humans have always relied on characteristics like facial structure or a person's voice to recognize those closest to them. But now biometrics is reaching new heights thanks to technology. It allows us to ID people through very specific traits—even those that aren't in plain sight, like the pattern of our veins.

It's hard to predict whether biometrics (and which ones) will become a common part of our daily lives. But there are a whole lot of people who believe that as technology advances, the time will come when you won't have to use a piece of ID to prove that you are you. Your body's physical characteristics or your behavioral traits will give you access to everywhere you want to go and everything you own. Some argue it's entirely possible that security passwords, documents proving identity, and even keys will become a thing of the past.

While many people stand firmly behind biometrics, it does have its share of opponents. There are concerns about the technology—from privacy issues to the fear of stolen biometric data to potential glitches that may put secure information or locations at risk. In spite of these worries, biometric technology shows no signs of slowing down.

So where is biometrics headed? It's anyone's guess, really. We've already taken a glimpse at some of the possibilities, like tongue biometrics, breathprints, and ... well, who can forget bum recognition! Experts are also investigating heartbeat rhythms and brainwave patterns to see if they could act as forms of ID. You just never know what's next. Someone may discover a way to use freckles as an identifier. Or perhaps our mad gaming skills and the way we use a controller may one day be used for identification. In biometrics, all it takes is for someone to discover a trait that's unique enough to confirm we are who we say we are.

As you learn about biometrics, it's only natural to be amazed by the technology and how easily it can identify you. But you should stop to marvel at yourself as well. Because when you put the technology aside, there's no denying what biometrics proves: from your fingernails to your breath to your pores to your gait, you are unique through and through.

INDEX

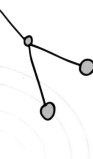

Acknowledgments:

Many thanks to everyone at Owlkids, especially Karen B., Karen L., Debbie, Judy, and Allison. And big thanks to my editor John Crossingham for your guidance from start to finish. Thank you to Ian Turner for your fantastic artwork, Danielle Arbour for your wonderful design work, and Janice Weaver for your helpful comments. My thanks to the Ontario Arts Council for your generous support of this project through the Writers' Reserve. Finally, thank you to Sam and Grace, who will always be the best part of me.

Biometric Solutions. "Fingerprint Recognition." 2016. Online.

Center for Biometrics and Security Research. "Biometrics." 2015. Online.

Chayka, Kyle. "Biometric Surveillance Means Someone is Always Watching You." Newsweek, 2014. Online.

CNN video; "How Iris Recognition Reads Your Eyes." video.cnn.org

Cofta, Piotr, Steven Furnell and Hazel Lacohée. *Understanding Public Perceptions*. Chicago: International Engineering Consortium, 2009.

De Chant, Tim. "The Boring and Exciting World of Biometrics." PBS.org, 2013. Online.

Glaser, April. "Biometrics Are Coming Along with Serious Security Concerns." Wired, 2016. Online.

Graham, Luke. "Biometrics: The Future of Digital Security." CNBC, 2016. Online.

Gregory, Peter H. and Michael A. Simon, *Biometrics for Dummies*. New Jersey: Wiley Publishers, 2008.

Griaule Biometrics. "History of Biometrics." 2014. Online.

Hall, Ronald. *Biometrics: 100 Most Asked Questions*. Brisbane: Emereo Publishing, 2012.

Lockie, Mark. *Biometric Technology*. Portsmouth: Heinemann Library, 2009.

Mayhew, Stephen. "History of Biometrics." Biometric Update, 2015. Online.

Moren, Dan. "7 Surprising Biometric Identification Methods." Popular Science, 2014. Online.

Rawlinson, Kevin. "Facial Recognition Technology: How Well Does it Work?" BBC News, 2015. Online.

Scientific American. "Biometric Security Poses Huge Privacy Risks." 2013. Online.

Singer, Natasha. "Never Forgetting a Face." The New York Times, 2014. Online.

Stastna, Kazi. "How Facial Recognition Technology is Creeping Into Daily Life." CBC News, 2014. Online.

Woodward, Jr., John D., Nicholas M. Orlans, Peter T. Higgins. *Biometrics*. New York: McGraw-Hill/Osborne, 2003.

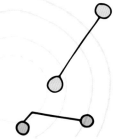